True if Not Destroyed

poems by

James Gage

Finishing Line Press
Georgetown, Kentucky

True if Not Destroyed

ACKNOWLEDGMENTS

I'd like to thank the following publications for first publishing these poems:

Apocalypse-Confidential: "The World Is Not Flat"
Dark Onus Lit: "Queensland Crocodile"
Mobius Magazine: "Elegy"
New Verse News: "Archipelago" & "Word"
Out of Line: "Wingman of the Gulf"
Oyster River Pages: "Coriolis, 2005"
PoemCity: "Mallaig"
PoemTown: "Boogaloo to Beck"
Powhatan Review: "Parchment"
Sand Hills Magazine: "Ernest N. Morial Convention Center, 2005"
Wordrunner: "Wake"

Publisher: Leah Huete de Maines
Editor: Christen Kincaid
Cover Art: James Gage
Author Photo: Lula Gage
Cover Design: James Gage

Order online: www.finishinglinepress.com
also available on amazon.com

Author inquiries and mail orders:
Finishing Line Press
PO Box 1626
Georgetown, Kentucky 40324
USA

Contents

"You can resolve to live your life through integrity. Let your credo be this:
Let the lie come into the world, let it even triumph.
But not through me.
The simple step of a courageous individual is
not to take part in the lie."
—Aleksandr Solzhenitsyn

♡

Hapgood Pond

The cramped preserver hatch
below the high lifeguard chair
squeezed us like a compress

as your emerald eyes flashed
and your lips warmed mine
and the musk of coconut oil

soaked the salt air.
Outside the dark love nest
of our beachside retreat

we could hear
the shrill whistles from
our teachers on the hill.

We giggled and kissed
and mined our last minutes,
mouths and hearts racing.

**

All these years since I can
still smell your skin and picture
your cheeks freckled and wet

like a palimpsest yet inscribed by
a lifetime. A patch of white
linen adrift on the wind.

Family Portrait

In front of the hearth. Pop off
to the right with Gram's layered
gaze crossing over his face
and out the porch window. She is
to his right, leg cocked behind him,
quick with pills and Preparation H.
His own posture is stooped
from polio and two bouts with
cancer, and his eyes seem to know
what his wife has been thinking.

My mother and teen brother
stand on each side behind me,
their eyes fixed expressions
like Verde Antique granite,
green-mottled and glazed.
My brother stares straight ahead,
wears a Yamaha mesh
three-quarter sleeve tee
fresh from the garage and his dirt bike
where Farrah in her red suit
smiles from the wall, teeth
gleaming down. In
our family portrait
my mother's own mouth is pursed
but her reasons for hating
her picture taken are different than
my brother's. Her right hand seizes
my shoulder. Rings dazzle.

Ten, I stand in tan Dickies
with my soft collar up
on a waffle-pique shirt.
My mother told me that
the alligators sold out at the mall
so she bought me a shirt
with a cat who is French.

Le Tigre, she says. That's you, tiger.

Mallaig

Not even the wind
nor the cliffs
nor the musk from the waves
when it's calm, balmy

you can taste it,
the sweet-smoke cells
of the Gulf Stream
and the peat meeting sea.

Down current from the south
it rolls over, your eyes
peer through pinched lids
and then finally tear up.

And that's when the malt
runs the gullet so well,
when the waterfalls empty
glaciers onto fossilized bones

before the mammoths and
ungulates, the hairy uprights
with their brows pressed together,
so proud above their new open flame.

The Disc Jockey

Flows at the sound of the
trombone, the slow baseline
of a French Quarter groove,
mood-hewn,
pedal down,
the screed of the B3.

Broad cheeks brightening
as a radiant smile
sets sail across her
pale moonstruck face—
eyes alight, ears on fire.

Helen of Granville

She works with
a cynic's progress—
deft-handed,
long generous strides
through the smoke-colored trees.

Skis, those ancient blades
forging ahead through the field—
always ahead, always further.
Arms racing legs,
face poised and flushed,
silent swaths and basket dots
on the wind-driven snow:
a canvas left smoldering
to show she was there.

Dream of the West
—for R.B., 7/21/27—11/5/10

My father stands at the wall and examines the lock.
Moving his fingers over the gilt edge to the glass
he traces the curves of the Mohawk in a framed painting
of the historic canal. Restored to its natural channel,
the flat current conceals its worn past: a dream of the west,
like my father had playing dominoes before the Second Great War.
Under the shade of a maple, in another part of the world.

Beneath the florescent lights of the VA lobby,
my father returns to his seat and closes his eyes. He dreams
of Kenton and Getz, of Horace Greeley and the horizon
blue line of the westward Pacific, of his own days
on the strand drinking daiquiris and jazz. He was twenty-seven
then. But now, a mottled blue light like silver tines in the sky
sends his heart keening and he awakens with a start
among a roomful of eyes. "The doctor will see you now."

So little to say since the sky was parsed out this morning.
In the elevator vets depict the inhuman events
in drilled bits of language as the steel car lifts higher.
A confessional smell presses in from all sides as the oldest
vet in the group mumbles under his breath "Bomb
the cocksuckers", silencing the rest.

All our histories are taught through the myopics of war,
a lesson my father first understood off the south shore of
Manhattan. A half-century hence, the doctor's cold
stethoscope searches his heart. Seventy-four,
he has outlasted Governor's Island and the Cold War
to face an empire's new fear, its unheralded power.
But his years are a salve for the solitude of yet,
a dream by stone-eyed engineers. Because walls
are like rivers—built to fall down—
forever in the minds of only their makers.

My father stares south out the window
and buttons his shirt. He recalls his
first trip to California and back,
driving young Teddy K.'s open-topped Pontiac

in the years before Dallas or dark Chappaquiddick.
He recalls Uncle Frank in the dustbowl of Yermo.
Old Uncle Frank, the long-recovering drunk, pointing to his wife
of forty-odd years, saying "She's the one who saved me."

He smiles as the elevator descends
and strides fast through the lobby
back out to the blue of this
new broken light lost in America.

Janjaweed

Laid out upon the baked desert floor
inside a circle thatch hut
a blind man stares up
through the white webbed
suns of his lids
and smiles to himself
as the voices outside
grow louder and clear.

He's heard these voices before—
the adrenaline rush
and peals of black laughter
that precede the children of obsidian,
red clay, the kids of the click-kill.

He once was one of them.

CNN, Sheep, Iraq

If I remove myself,
deep-six my convictions
and head back to the forty,
will this drone of white noise
finally cease and desist,
will the truth in my mind
reconcile with the lies?

The loss is unknowable and
the numbers don't lie,
and these war dead
suffuse through our lives
by the mere blink of a screen.
We are meant
to believe them, believe in them—

these cable ken dolls
and collagen queens,
their unceasing smiles
and vernacular ease
designed to numb our best senses.
The cause and effect of complacence,
the taut ring of a skin drum beating alone.

Bombs, beheadings,
maimings on Main Street,
the endless soundbyte from
the hard-ons at Enzyte—
it's all the same circle,
a commercial, then news.

A lens to help separate us from our thoughts,
a blade forged to emasculate,
a path that will lead us to slaughter.

Wingman of the Gulf

for Petty Officer Third Class Stephen K. Rand

I can only imagine
what you first understood
on those blast iron floors of the ship
with surveillance photos
splayed out like ordnance,
like the flat death
they would later become. Did your mind

flash for an instant to some distant memory,
some nursery rhyme moment
forgotten from youth?
Did your twenty-two years
begin to feel like a sieve,
like some filter for existence
with no clear beginning and without any end?

In the recruitment office
you hadn't heard the word death
but of course there were signs,
and the synonyms replayed in your mind
what you hoped you could be:
heroic and brave, invincible, best.
War was just an abstraction,
a stop-cycle thought that happened to
somebody else, but then there you were:

green and clean-shaven,
co-ordinate seeker,
eye-dropper of bombs.

In your nursery room dreams
did the sheep have brave faces
as they met their demise, and did they have names?
Did they bleat out real words as they
moved between worlds in that deja-vu instant
when the sky was blot out?
What was then left

to replace that small word
which has no earthly meaning,
and what could be done with the nothing
that remained?

What could be gleaned from history's lesson
unlearned, and what shape would it take—
this divisive and spiteful

utter blindness of
faith?

The World Is Not Flat

In another part of the world
your eyes which are worn
will be torn from their sockets
and bejeweled on a cane
to be dipped in the amber
of an ancestral tree, this by
decree of some misconceived god,
mohammed, jesus, et cetera.

In another part of the world
your hair which is blessed
will be braided for rope
atop Olduvai Gorge
where the natives stand watch
outside the colonel's mud hut
and his bone-latticed village
and his unwaving dead.

In another part of the world
where the names are still
scratched into rocks
of long-forgotten black wells,
where the cotton remains
and the coal ash rings fade—
such is the fate of
a species at war.

Archipelago

"To do evil a human being must first believe that what he is doing is good."
-Alexander Solzhenitsyn

Torture is a word
with more than four letters
but of course there are worse, words

like earlobe or gulag or Bagram
Air Base, places you hoped your
concealment might keep you from seeing.

*

It has been more than ten years
since Alexander returned to the taiga,
forty-some seasons since
he left us for dusk and the world
is the same now but different,
the appeals have grown louder.
The courts have drawn down
their heavyweight robes and butterflies
are trapped in their vestments.
The bailiff keeps checking his watch.

Still the old man sits
in the back of the room
and stares stalwartly on,
beard spilling from his eyes
like silver tailings from a mine,
he is quiet, there is too much to say
and he's already said it, bellowed from
the hemlocks and his solitary cells

against the fear and the hate
for the hope and the love
without raising his voice,
without raising his hand.

*

Through ribboning birch
the snow hums down like an iron
branding on skin. A voice rings out
and then fades, swallowed by
a silence that spreads like an inkblot.

13

Boogaloo to Beck

When the flags catch fire
from the flame-licked pickets
and the trigger-fixed sheep
bleat raptured applause
as they crash to the ground,
bound by the compacts
of the broken and old,
slave-wrought South
and the capitalized North—

only then will we know
how the war was unwon.

Among the cynics and prophets
with their pitchforks and Glocks
screaming once and for all
how our gods have withdrawn

and how crazy Ron Hubbard
was actually right,
cackling black teeth
from a celestial grave:

You don't get rich writing science fiction.
If you want to get rich, you start a religion.

♡

Wake

Curbside by the Tyler
under Vedder's low roar:
Black, and the histrionics of night.
And us—another roadside drama
revealed by the backslide of love.

But what love we made
on that last holdover morning,
a carnal vernacular
among colonial ghosts.
They must have known
we would come together
in that battle-stained house,
your caterwauling screams astride
my own guttural rush—white knuckled,
the way it's always been
with lovers diffused, with lovers forced
to find their own way.

These songs of the heart
are immutable, vernal,
utterly mortal.
Sing now
in the wake of what's lost.

Tureen

I love to raise you up with my hands
like a wide shallow soup bowl
by the backs of your thighs
slowly forward,

my tureen
I am pulling you
closer till your nectar
meets my parched lips

my mouth
finding its way
to your

soft scented essence

a sugar sublime as your
hips in their quiver and
your body its shudder
in the mute morning light
toward our slumbering peace.

Purgatory

It is hard to recall
the turning of the desert
as it fell from your eyes,
the stark burnished blue
that guided us
through those four-cornered years
as you smiled over your shoulder
and I raced behind.

Beyond the clay-bitten dusk
and the firelit mesa
the La Platas beckoned to us
like a mirage inching closer
than we ever could.
The unbidden moon rose
over white stucco walls
as a solitary wolf threaded
through the naked scrub pines.

It was there, so far from the east
where we loved and lost passion,
a moment of stridence
as the umber light fades.

Parchment

Of course it's just memory
that finds me forgotten and wet
these seasons back from your heart.

I'm soaked, forlorn,
entranced by your smile
like some new form of Braille:
a snapshot I've hung above others—
that kiss on the Winhall,
this need in the dark.

Even now over these washboard roads
your voice springs to my mind
like a billet-doux—
gravid with intention, soft with allure.
Elusive: a page torn from the past
but dog-eared, with notes
scratched hard in the margins.

Maybe you're like that
dream of the sun-dance, that
Cerulean sky etched without clouds.
But then maybe the clouds
color you whole.

Gut of Vermont

How will the future perceive
this unique human moment, this
precarious rain and barium sky,
these black rubber blades
cleaving curve-tempered glass
as I drive slowly north
between Taconics and Greens.

Having just left my friend
the benevolent Berry
and his wife Carol
who bring seasons of passion
of vee-dreaming geese,
flocks of bright birds
over fields of Van Gogh.
And now passing through town
where Superman's father
once led a bookclub in the '90's
before his son's terrible fall.

And still there is solace
found in the rocks
of the Old Stone Shop
branding Hubbardton Forge,
or in Veterans Park,
or the book I don't know
but never forgot.

On my childhood drift
up the gut of Vermont.

Prayer for a Parent

Every day around four it gets dark.
It doesn't matter the season
or the weather outside

or the way the cup holder light
strikes the mirror in the hall
as you shuffle by slowly.

You find yourself on your phone
scrolling through texts,
always hoping to read a few words

from the one true voice of your daughter.
On the web there are groups
for parents captured by absence,

and it's a peculiar form of grief
that gets posted online
since these children are not

gone from this world, but merely
withheld. And though unbothered exes
help deliver the silence,

they are guided by lights that
flash from the dashboard of a culture
destroyed, designed to divide

and then conquer
pathologized parents
still keening from loss.

At dusk you awaken, black glass
on your knee in the sarcophagus
of your car. The smell

of smoked peat and the
leaves drifting down
soon blanket the windshield.

Occupation of the American Mind

At fifteen sex and death were
as foreign to me as an Afghan wedding,
sun-bleached and formless,
a veil suddenly lifted now filled with air.
At fifteen the passion I remembered best
was the kiss, the gut-love of memory
beyond the rock wall or beneath the still water.

Do you know what they showed us on the TV last night?
That homage to Onan, *Victoria's Secret*,
and there I sat in full testicular splendor—
one hand on the couch back,
the other hand on my cock. I even got misty.
I'm sorry—does my language offend you?
I can stick with metaphors if you like,
you always liked metaphors like you liked your TV.
It always kept you from thinking
about words like *dismember*, about people like me.

So there you were again angel, aiming your way down.
I could see the taut milkweeds in the
lines drawn behind you, but then
how does it go? *My disbelief was suspended,*
like yours in midair. Your ass looked spectacular.

And that's when I felt my own marionette
strings snap back into place
and I sat prone in my cell,
silently rubbing my eyes. I took a deep
breath and peered through the lens,
then began shooting again.

Because there is no heaven
and there are no fucking angels.
Those seventy-two virgins were a figment.

Ernest N. Morial Convention Center, 2005

It's a smoke
    salt
        shitshow
off Canal Street
with this stream
of black catcalls
that just never stops,
these thin rubber soles
that slap at the treads
of the non-escalating stairs.

Two boys in their teens
appear out of the dark,
features concealed
beneath cycloptic
headlamps aimed
toward the weakest
among us—the elders and infirm,
the toddlers hunched with their mothers
below patchwork quilts or Glad plastic bags,

all of us waiting

for some glimmer of light
to return before morning.

A cellphone snaps shut,
the boys move down the hall.
The night air stills around us—
a salve and a friend, a mortified wound.

Coriolis, 2005

Get up, country.

New Orleans is calling collect
but George Jr. chewed through
the cord so the charge is reversed
and the answer's still no.

Go ahead and read the note
at the end of the dock: gone fishing
for lunch, with Rove in the Gulf
where it's all bluefin and craps
and neocon Noahs on Moby patrol.

Up there's Trent Lott, cocked in the
crows' nest and laughing, snapping
bottlecaps at Condi as she lines up
her shot. Starboard,
hundreds of miles
from the eye of the storm
they'll dine on fish eggs & clam bellies,
tenderloin lamb with a neon mint glaze,
sip Cristal from a Waterford glass.

Meanwhile onshore
you're still mired in shit,
in the sewer of Canal Street
as we watch through the screen
from the satellite dish. Get up, country.

Fire your President.

Elegy

My country
right or wrong.

Wrong.

Queensland Crocodile

In my dream I can't recall
how many sets of teeth you have
but I can see row upon row

flashing the sun's rays following
the salt rush of the flood.
Your fine and sharp

incisors glistening
in the new light.
An opportunist, you

stand on the street grinning.
As Darwinian as your genes or
your mother Komodo twice

removed. I should have
expected your reptile
heart would devastate

and it does. It protects
in the way it betrays:
with certitude and pride

and a bent for revenge.
It is small consolation
to know you're

a scourge for evolution,
as Australian as a Brit
prisoner killing an aborigine,

or a croc swallowing
a dog. You are as American
as a Remington

aimed unto slaves,
and you are
human as fuck.

Slate, Fate

"If you can't solve a problem, make it bigger."
—Donald Rumsfeld

By proxy we bomb,
light up the sky and trail
our support through
this thin vale of tears—
a pre-emptive strike
to pre-empt the night,
the only thing left
when there's nothing else left
but this dust-driven slate, fate,
grey chemtrails to gone.

Because it's just a quick click
from the sandbox of Vegas
to the peaks of Tehran,
a carpal tunnel flex through
the haze of the playground
where the seesaws settle
below mushrooming flames,
interminable roar—
thirty-third degree eunuchs
dreaming black dawn.

♡

Hope/Fact

From the mouth of the Gila we flew
over legions of geckos and radial plains
to the unceasing fount
all the way back to the source,

my pen scribing time
as I read you our books
charting The Adventures of Curious George
and the Cactus Hotel,
the Lupine Lady and her dubious charms.

The prism of youth flashed before you,
your sole centered gaze
like a fly on a string
found comfort in trees
green yet unburdened,
and your fears fell behind.

Or that's been the hope.

Moon

Even as an infant,
your mind and heart flew
wide open. Squinting and
silent you would stare
out through the bars
of your heirloom oak crib
and listen to the groans
of our old Victorian, ever vigilant
for the thundering steps of
your brother the toddler,
that errant dive-bomber
and sometime protector of you.

Later at Dartmouth I watched
your eyes watching, racing
behind lids now firmly closed.
The pediatrician soothed us
with no cause for concern
amidst all the maps and the capillaries,
the synapse of your parents
and their unblinking eyes.

I know that I'm pleading here. It is just
that I want you to know
there is no one above and
no one below.

Just you, and your love,
and everything you choose.

Snow Globe

The first snow in the year of your birth
was a pelting hail in October, two weeks
before a pale Halloween.

You were four months old then
and developing a laugh, rocking hard
to roll over. We called you names:
Biggie-Biggie, Guapito.
We kissed you with fervor.

In the year of your birth we were learning
the little things, the things that most mattered.
And though the skirmish of the world
perched uneasy outside
our own house was buoyant,
untethered and ready
to sail off through the void.
High above our little village
sky-whitened with snow
we squinted through glass—
that diamond is where you'll play baseball,
that river you'll swim,
that mountain you'll climb.

***

When I finally awoke
you stood in the door frame
apart from the others
holding take-out
in a double-wrapped bag.
You had been pacing,
but now you were still.

"How's the old goat? Hungry?"
You walked over and slapped a hand
on the bed, tore open the bag.
"Not yet," I said.

You twirled a strand of lo mein
on a black plastic fork.

"Remember to bend," I thought you said.

I paused.

"The PT lady comes around in the mornings," I answered.

You chuckled.

"No, I meant Oregon—Mt. Bachelor.
That spring with Big Fuego."

You fed yourself another fork full of noodles.

I looked up at the ceiling, at the cracked latex paint
in the corners, and remembered
our first day on that dormant volcano:
the electric stillness of the woods
with the flakes floating down,
our tight powder turns and adrenaline
yelps. A morning of benevolence following
our fight the night prior—your explosion of ego,
my hackneyed response.

You stopped eating and
pulled at your hat, a grey
ushanka with rabbit fur flaps.

I heard a sigh come
from another part of the room
and I soon fell asleep.

Cloward-Piven Revisited

No words from the dashcam clips
titled *Streets of Philadelphia*
What happened today,
just the muted street sounds
and Market line rush scoring
car window footage of
humans junked up on the sidewalks
block after block,
contorted bent frames
only previously seen
in black-and-white footage
of corpses from war.

Stooped and slow moving
in gray Puma hoodies
and torn-at-the knee jeans
hiding sunken-lit eyes and
deepening lesions with the
bone-tin clang of the El overhead
just a few miles from Frank's metal bell
as the Xylazine zombies
chew torn heels of pizza
hunkered down over needles
now prostrate, now totally gone.

Under the green iron husk
of the outbound T
the crush of the junction
grows quiet in the din
beyond Kensington & H.

Lahaina

It has been a year since
the wildfires on Maui
and the net is bereft
amidst the sudden blue roofs
and the lies and half-truths
unremittingly hidden,
adrift and obscured
on the broken world web.

Silence on the home pages
of the puppets online—
no stories on the thirty day
mark from the mastheads
at the Times or at Fox or
Billy G.'s NBC.

No photos of the mesh now
lashed to the miles
of chained links
hiding Front Street
as the unmarked cars
guard the borders
of the barren steel fence.
            No voices from the kids
now drowned in the harbor
amidst black lava rocks
of this slave island holdout
that Rosa Koire
once warned us about.

A wish rolled into a bottle
as the sun smoulders down
on the blue-eyed Pacific.

Words

"Thinking your mind was my own in a dream." —Neil Young, 1972
"They can have Rogan or Young. Not both." —Young, fifty years later

Word is the best
four-letter word
of them all—
the most truly inclusive
and the least obscene.

I prefer the sound
of true voices
speaking to each other
with the gift of our forebears:
the bilabial smacks
and long glottal stops,
the carefully wrought thoughts
in place of wild haste
or wind-driven spasms.

In the end it is only our language
beyond mere evolution,
the harnessing of fire
or the plunger-dropped shot.
Beyond the silencing of words
lies the birdsong of love.

www.ingramcontent.com/pod-product-compliance
Lightning Source LLC
Chambersburg PA
CBHW030052100426
42734CB00038B/1268